# Love, Dad

## by Patrick Connolly

## by Patrick Connolly

**A Father's Daily Epistles to His Two Boys ...
Written on the Run and Left on the Breakfast Table**

**Andrews, McMeel & Parker**
A Universal Press Syndicate Company
**Kansas City • New York**

ISBN: 0-8362-7927-1
Library of Congress Catalog Card Number: 85-71928

First Printing, July 1985
Fourth Printing, May 1986

---
#### Attention: Schools and Businesses

## Foreword

*Note: This letter was written to Pat Connolly's wife, Laura, after his death. Written in hindsight, it nevertheless provides an insightful introduction to* Love, Dad.


En Route to Los Angeles
February 27, 1984


Laura —
   There isn't a day or an hour that goes by that I don't wish I could talk to Pat, to laugh with him again, to slap him on the back, and tell him that I love him and let him know I care —

In so many ways he was so much more successful in his career than I've been. And despite the minor problems (and they were minor) in the bureau, he was happy there — and he was appreciated there. The red-rimmed eyes I saw in church attest to this — there was no one in the bureau who was not *deeply* affected by Pat's passing.

Pat was a very important part of the heart and soul of my life and the life of the AP. And the lives of the AP staffers he worked with. He made the AP a better service. A much, much better service, because he told stories that truly touched people and enlightened them. And, so very often, made them happy. He was the *best* writer and reporter I've ever worked with.

Today, it's as if a painting has fallen from its frame, and you're left looking at an incredible patch of white space.

There's a prayer the Makah Indians say: if you have not heard it, I'd like to share it with you because I think it captures the way Pat felt —

Do not stand at my grave and weep.
I am not there. I do not sleep.
I am a thousand winds that blow.

I am the diamond glint on snow.
I am the sunlight on ripened grain.
I am the gentle autumn rain.

When you wake in the morning hush
I am the swift, uplifting rush
Of quiet birds in circling flight.
I am the soft starlight at night.

Do not stand at my grave and weep.
I am not there. I do not sleep.

With all my very best,

*John*

John C. Brewer
Chief of the Los Angeles
Associated Press Bureau

# CAST OF CHARACTERS

MOM

RICH

DAVE

COUGAR "Wonderdog!!"

Dad

DAVE AND RICH —
THIS IS A BRAND NEW,
ENTIRELY FRESH
COMPLETELY UNUSED,
JUST-OFF-THE-ASSEMBLY LINE
WEEK.

USE IT WELL.

DON'T RIDE IT
OVER A CLIFF
OR OFF THE
END OF A DOCK.

IT'S A FIRST-CLASS WEEK
THAT WILL STAND UP TO
A LOT OF USE, BUT NOT ABUSE.

IT'S THE KIND OF WEEK
YOU CAN DO WHEELIES ON,
IF YOU'RE CAREFUL.

YOU CAN BOUNCE BALLS
ON IT, PLAY JUMBOES ON
IT AND RUN ON IT WITH
YOUR NEW SHOES. YOU CAN
SPLASH IN IT, TOO. WHAT
A GREAT WEEK!

YOU CAN USE IT AS A BOOKMARK
TO HELP YOU STUDY, OR TO SIT ON
WHILE YOU READ. IT'S A GOOD WEEK
TO FLUFF UP LIKE A PILLOW AND
PUT UNDER YOUR HEAD WHEN YOU NAP --- OR
TO THROW BACK AND FORTH ON THE PLAYGROUND.
YOU CAN PLAY THIS WEEK IN YOUR TRUMPET,
OR ROLLERSKATE ON IT. WHAT A WONDERFUL
VERSATILE WEEK IF YOU USE IT RIGHT!

LOVE,
Dad

DAVE AND RICH —
HAPPY LAST DAY
OF SUMMER VACATION!
At Last you can go back
to school.

ALL SUMMER you have
been learning from Personal
experience, which means
you did the things you learned
about, LIKE turning bales and
VISITING SITTING BULL'S GRAVE.

In School you will also learn
from Books, which requires
imagination and concentration.
You will also learn Many skills,
such as mathematics and reading,
which will make the world a more
interesting, more understandable
place to live.

LOVE,
Dad

GOOD MORNING,
GOOD GUYS !!!
WELCOME BACK
TO SCHOOL !
IT'S GOING TO BE
A GREAT YEAR
FOR YOU BOTH.
LEARNING THINGS
YOU NEVER KNEW BEFORE
AND SHARING
YOUR KNOWLEDGE
WITH OTHERS.
THIS IS THE START
OF A WHOLE NEW
PART OF YOUR LIVES,
A BRAND NEW ADVENTURE
FULL OF EXCITEMENT,
NEW FRIENDS, NEW THINGS
TO DO. I SORT OF ENVY
YOU FOR ALL THAT.
I don't have a bunch
of advice--except to
say, "DO WHAT YOU KNOW IS
RIGHT, EVEN IF IT'S THE
HARD THING SOMETIMES."
HAVE A WONDERFUL DAY AND YEAR
LOVE, Dad

Dave and Rich
HERE ARE SOME RULES
FOR FORMAL DINING

DO NOT PUT YOUR ELBOWS
IN YOUR MASHED POTATOES. →

WHEN YOU DINE WITH YOUR
PINKY UP, BE CAREFUL OF IT.

IF YOU CHOOSE TO LEAVE
ONE HAND ON YOUR LAP,
LOOK AROUND TO MAKE
SURE THERE IS NOT A
HUNGRY DOG NEARBY.

LOVE,
Dad

DAVE AND RICH,
WE SURE ENJOYED
YOUR COMPANY LAST
NIGHT.

QUESTION: DO YOU KNOW WHAT'S
SPECIAL ABOUT TODAY
IN HISTORY?

ANSWER: IT IS THE 100TH ANNIVERSARY
OF THE BIRTH OF ALBERT EINSTEIN.
HE WAS A FAMOUS MATHEMATICIAN
AND THEORIST WHOSE IDEAS
CHANGED OUR OWN IDEAS ABOUT
THE UNIVERSE.

(BY THE WAY, PEOPLE THOUGHT
EINSTEIN WAS KIND OF SLOW
IN SCHOOL!)

"SOMETIMES I STILL
COUNT ON MY FINGERS
TO MAKE SURE
I'M RIGHT."

HE DEVISED THEORIES
ABOUT SPACE AND TIME,
HOW THE UNIVERSE
EXPANDS, HOW GRAVITY
WORKS, WHY ATOMS CAN
BE "SPLIT" FOR
ENERGY, AND WHY
LIGHT TRAVELS 186,283
MILES PER SECOND.
HE ONCE WROTE TO A STUDENT
WHO WAS HAVING TROUBLE IN
SCHOOL, "DO NOT WORRY
ABOUT YOUR DIFFICULTIES
IN MATHEMATICS; I CAN
ASSURE YOU MINE ARE
STILL GREATER."
DAVE and RICH, REMEMBER
ALBERT EINSTEIN.
LOVE,
Dad

DAVE AND RICH,
WELL, HAPPY BIRTHDAY, RICH.
ELEVEN YEARS OLD... THAT'S
MORE THAN A DECADE. YOU'VE
LIVED THROUGH A WHOLE
DECADE. IT'S CALLED
"THE '70s." BY THE TIME
"THE '80s" ARE OVER, YOU'LL
BE IN YOUR 20s.

ALL THOSE NUMBERS ARE
STARTING TO SOUND CONFUSING...
ANYWAY, WE ALL WISH YOU
A HAPPY BIRTHDAY!

DAVE, WE DIDN'T FORGET YOU.
HAPPY UNBIRTHDAY!!

"I LIKE CANDLES..."

...THAT DOESN'T
BY CHANCE
MEAN I GET
AN
UNBIRTHDAY
PRESENT,
DOES IT?

love,
Dad

Dave and Rich,

THIS IS A FISHING LESSON SO REMEMBER IT WELL:

THIS ENTIRE LARGE PART OF THE BRAIN IS THE CEREBRUM. IT HELPS YOU REASON. THAT MEANS IT HELPS YOU DECIDE THINGS LIKE WHETHER TO GO FISHING, WHERE TO FISH AND WHAT KIND OF BAIT TO USE.

THIS LITTLE PART BACK HERE IS THE CEREBELLUM. IT RUNS PARTS OF YOUR BODY, LIKE THE HANDS, FEET, EYES, EARS, ORGANS, ALL THE MOVING PARTS. WHEN YOUR CEREBRUM DECIDES TO REEL IN A FISH, YOUR CEREBELLUM MAKES YOUR HANDS WORK TO DO IT. OF COURSE, AS YOU KNOW, THE CEREBELLUM ALSO DOES THINGS YOU DON'T EVEN THINK ABOUT, LIKE MAKE YOUR HEART BEAT ALL DAY AND NIGHT YOUR WHOLE LIFE.

I THINK YOU SHOULD KNOW ALL THIS FISHING INFORMATION BEFORE YOU GO DOWN TO THE PIER.

LOVE,
Dad.

HELLO, LITTLE FELLOWS.
symbols are Things
That stand for other
Things.
For instance, the symbol
Fe stands for iron. IT's
not really iron. IT WOULD BE
MESSY carrying around real
iron Every time you wanted to
write about iron. It is much
simpler to use a symbol for
iron.
We see symbols all around us.
The "Arrow of Light" is a symbol
of many Achievements by a scout.
IT is not The achievements Themselves,
but a symbol representing them.
words and letters are symbols. The
word "ELEPHANT" is not a real elephant.
IT is a group of letters organized to
symbolize an elephant. Having a
real elephant around whenever you
talk about elephants would
BE Messy.

HELLO,
LITTLE
FELLOWS.

Can you tell Mom some
other symbols?

LOVE,
Dad
symbol for
Dad

ALSO A
SYMBOL

DAVE AND RICH ~
GOOD MORNING.
IT'S RAINING HARD.
YOU CAN HEAR THE
DROPS PLASHING ON
THE PATIO ROOF.

I HEARD A MOTHER
ROBIN WARN HER
BABY ROBIN TO STAY
IN THE SHALLOW END
OF THE YARD!

LOVE,
Dad

Dave and Rich —

Be good in school today.

By that I don't mean get good grades.

I mean, behave yourselves.

Good grades are nice and you should shoot for them.

But the way to get ahead is to behave.

Love,
Dad

DAVE AND RICH,
DID YOU EVER GET THE FEELING THAT COUGAR IS TEACHING US NEW TRICKS?
"THAT'S REAL GOOD, FELLOWS. COUGAR MUST BE PROUD OF YOU."
LOVE, Dad

Dave and Rich,
Good Morning. it's a
New day. God gives
us new days so we
can continue with
our successes or
start over if we
goofed yesterday.

Mom and I love You.
You're very important little people.

Have a good friday.

love,
Dad

I'M IMPORTANT,
TOO, IN MY
OWN WAY...

Dave and Rich,
Just a quick note today.

You must be about ready to go back to school.

Vacations are nice for a little change of pace but a guy really needs the hard work of the classroom to stay in shape.

Love,
Dad

Dave and Rich,

EVEN A LONG
WEEKEND GOES
FAST, DOESN'T IT?
SCHOOL ISN'T EXACTLY
A VACATION. IT IS MORE
LIKE AN ADVENTURE,
WHERE YOU GO
EXPLORING THROUGH YOUR
WORLD AND MAKING ALL
KINDS OF DISCOVERIES.
ABOUT THINGS LIKE MATH, HISTORY,
MUSIC, FOREIGNERS, ART, GEOGRAPHY,
GEOLOGY, GRAVITY, LANGUAGE, ALL
THE TEXTURES AND COLORS OF YOUR
EARTH, FROM TINY THINGS TOO SMALL
TO SEE TO GIANTS, LIKE DINOSAURS!

WHAT LUCK TO BE HEADED OFF
ON ANOTHER EXPEDITION
TOMORROW!

LOVE,

Dad...

... DOWN,
COUGAR!

COUGAR RIDING
WITH KIDS ON THE
WAY BACK FROM
REDGATE.

GOOD MORNING,
Dave and Rich.

I hope You two
have an interesting,
Exciting day in school.
Rich, Pay close attention
on the field day so You
can tell Mom and I
Everything You learn.

"I'LL TELL YOU GUYS
A SECRET.
DINOSAURS ARE
NOT HUGE,
DINOSAURS ARE
REGULAR SIZE.
PEOPLE JUST THINK
WE'RE HUGE
BECAUSE PEOPLE
ARE SO TINY."

LOVE,
Professor Father

DAVE & RICH —

WHEN I EAT MY APRICOTS
TODAY, I'LL THINK OF MOM
AND YOU GUY'S PEELING
THEM ALL.

AND WHEN I READ AND WRITE,
I'LL THINK OF YOU TWO IN SCHOOL,
LEARNING HOW TO GROW UP.

GROWING UP DOESN'T MEAN GETTING TALLER.
IT DOESN'T MEAN WEARING SPECIAL CLOTHES.
IT DOESN'T MEAN HANGING AROUND
WITH JUST THE POPULAR KIDS AND
IGNORING EVERYBODY ELSE.

GROWING UP MEANS LEARNING
TO BE HONEST WITH YOURSELF.

GROWING UP MEANS WORKING
HARD WHEN THERE'S WORK TO DO —
AND PLAYING HARD WHEN THERE'S
PLAYING TO DO.

GROWING UP MEANS BEING FAIR
TO EVERYBODY.

IT MEANS LEARNING TO LAUGH
AT YOURSELF, NOT AT OTHER PEOPLE.

GROWING UP MEANS KNOWING YOU
ARE GOING TO MAKE MISTAKES
BECAUSE NOBODY'S PERFECT —— AND
ADMITTING MISTAKES WHEN YOU MAKE
THEM.

MOM & I LOVE YOU GUY'S. YOU HAVE A GOOD
START AT GROWING UP. KEEP AT IT.

LOVE, Dad

Dave and Rich,
I KNOW IT'S GOING TO BE A GOOD DAY. THE SUN IS BRIGHT AND WARM, THE BIRDS ARE SINGING (COUNTRY & WESTERN, I THINK), COUGAR IS RACING AROUND TO SEE WHO IS UP AND WHAT MISCHIEF SHE CAN GET INTO AND MOM HAS HER EARS PERKED UP, LISTENING FOR FLOWERS GROWING.

Dave, I THINK IN A SHORT TIME you can memorize THE REST OF THE CAPITALS TODAY.

RICH, I THINK you can work on some MATH.

HARK! I HEAR A RHODODENDRON COMING!

See you later
LOVE, Dad

KIDS,

GOOD MORNING, YOU TWO.
HELP MOM OUT TODAY.
RICH, IT WAS GRATIFYING
TO SPRING A HOMONYM
ON YOU AND FIND OUT
YOU KNOW IT (AS IN
PAUSE AND PAWS YESTERDAY).

DAVE, YOUR TRUMPET
IS SOUNDING A LITTLE
LOUDER AND A LITTLE
CLEARER.
BOTH OF YOU KEEP UP THE
GOOD WORK.

LOVE,
Dad

DEAR KIDS,
IT IS EARLY,
EARLY IN THE
MORNING. THE
SUN HASN'T EVEN
STARTED COMING UP
AND THERE ARE
HARDLY ANY PEOPLE
AROUND. EVEN THE
BIRDS ARE STILL
ASLEEP. THE ONLY
SOUND IS MOTHER'S
SOFT FOOTSTEPS
IN THE KITCHEN
AND THE COFFEE
PERKING. IN A
FEW MINUTES, THE
FIRST SUN'S RAYS
WILL APPEAR AND
THE WORLD WILL
START TO STIR.
UNTIL THEN, MOM
AND I HAVE IT
ALMOST ALL TO
OURSELVES.
VERY EARLY
MORNING IS ONE
OF THE BEST
TIMES OF DAY.

LOVE,
Dad

DAVE AND RICH,

I HOPE YOU BOTH HAVE A GOOD DAY. REMEMBER TO LEARN SOMETHING NEW AND NOT TO FORGET THE OLD STUFF. YOU HAVE ROOM TO STORE ALL THAT INFORMATION IN YOUR HEAD. YOUR BRAIN IS LIKE AN ATTIC WHERE YOU STORE CLOTHES AND TOYS AND OLD FURNITURE AND BOOKS. EXCEPT INSTEAD OF THINGS, YOU STORE IDEAS, WHICH ARE MUCH MORE VALUABLE.

LOVE,

Dad

DAVE AND RICH,

- DO YOUR WORK.

- BE RESPONSIBLE FOR YOURSELVES.

- TAKE PRIDE IN YOUR ACCOMPLISHMENTS.

- TRY HARD.

- LOVE YOUR FRIENDS, FAMILY, YOURSELVES AND EVEN STRANGERS.

- TELL THE TRUTH.

Love,
Dad

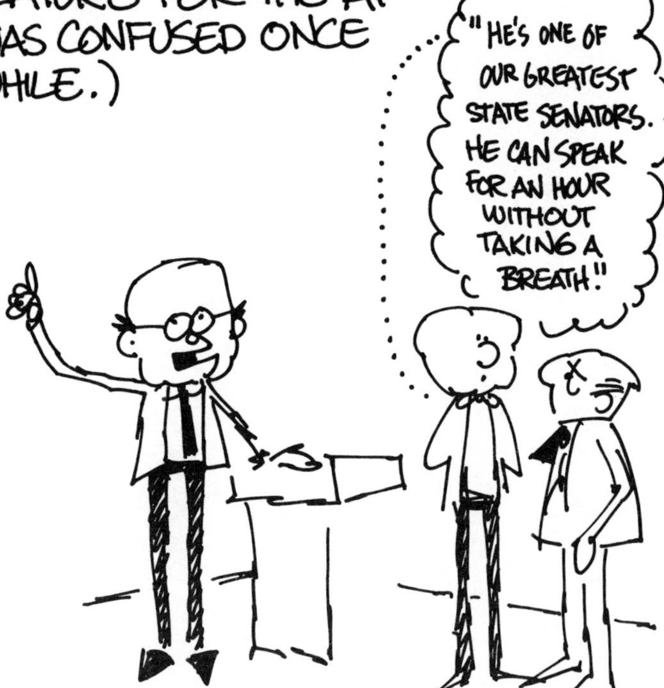

DAVE AND RICH

TODAY IS
GENERAL ELECTION DAY.
WE CHOOSE WHO GOVERNS US
AND WE CHOOSE SOME OF THE
RULES WE LIVE BY, WHICH
ARE CALLED "INITIATIVES"
AND "REFERENDUMS" ON
THE BALLOT.
   MOM AND I ARE GOING TO VOTE.
ELECTION DAY IS IMPORTANT.
Voting is the only way to
get some things done.
   If we don't cast ballots,
we can't complain about
the Government.
                        Love,
                         Dad

DAVE AND RICH ~

IT'S RAINING BUT
THE BIRDS ARE CHIRPING.

IT MUST BE A LITTLE LIKE
SINGING IN THE SHOWER.

LA LA LA LA LA LA

DAVE, RUN THROUGH SOME OF
THE IRREGULAR ADJECTIVES
AND ADVERBS WITH MOM.

RICH, HOW DO YOU SPELL
THE CONTRACTION OF
"THEY ARE"?

LOVE,
Dad

DAVE AND RICH—
GOOD MORNING.
THE DALAI LAMA
IS FROM TIBET.
QUICK, FIND TIBET
ON THE MAP. MOM WILL
HELP YOU. MAYBE THE
COUNTRY IS NOT MARKED,
BECAUSE IT WAS ABSORBED
BY THE CHINESE, BUT THE
CAPITAL CITY IS THERE. IT
IS CALLED LHANSA. IT IS
HIGH IN THE HIMALAYAN
MOUNTAINS BETWEEN CHINA
AND INDIA. TIBET WAS
CALLED "THE ROOFTOP OF THE
WORLD". WHY? TELL ME WHEN
I GET HOME. THE CHINESE
COMMUNISTS KILLED MANY
TIBETANS IN 1959 AND THE
DALAI LAMA HAD TO FLEE FOR
HIS LIFE. HE WOULD LIKE TO GO
BACK HOME, BUT ONLY IF THE
COMMUNISTS WILL BE GOOD
TO HIS PEOPLE AND LET THEM
ALONE. MOST OF THE SIX
MILLION TIBETANS BELIEVE
THE DALAI LAMA IS GOD, AS
WELL AS BEING KING. SO HE
IS SACRED TO MANY PEOPLE,
LIKE JESUS IS SACRED TO US.
HE IS A VERY HOLY MAN WHO
WANTS TO GO HOME TO HIS
PEOPLE AND DO GOOD
TO THEM.

LOVE,
Dad

READ THIS
OUT LOUD TO
MOM.

THE
DALAI LAMA
WILL BE IN
SEATTLE THURSDAY
AND FRIDAY.

THE
DALAI LAMA
SHAVES HIS
HEAD TO BE
HUMBLE. HE
TENDS TO SMILE
BECAUSE HE IS
PEACEFUL.

THE WORDS
"DALAI LAMA"
MEAN IN MONGOLIAN
LANGUAGE, "OCEAN
OF WISDOM".

DAVE AND RICH,

WELL, YOU'RE HEADING
BACK TO SCHOOL AGAIN
AFTER A LONG ACTIVE
WEEKEND FILLED WITH THE
ZOO, A WATERFRONT
DINNER OF FISH AND CHIPS,
FAT TUESDAY AND
ROLLERSKATING.

WHILE YOU'RE IN SCHOOL,
STUDY AS HARD AS YOU
PLAYED. STUDY HARDER.
MAKE IT A CONTEST
WITH YOURSELF TO SEE
IF YOU CAN STUDY
HARDER THAN YOU
PLAYED.

MOM AND I LOVE YOU.
I'LL SEE YOU TWO
GOOD GUYS TONIGHT.

LOVE,

DAVE + RICH

OKAY, WE'LL HAVE A
LITTLE QUIZ
HERE FROM PROFESSOR
CONNOLLY:

← WHAT TYPE OF ANGLE IS THIS?

140°

47° WHAT ABOUT THIS?

180° OR THIS?

EACH IS A TYPE OF ANGLE THAT HAS A SPECIFIC NAME.

Hey, You Guys, Dave and Rich, and
Beautiful, Kind, Loving, Smart, Crafty,
Wonderful MOM, I LOVE You.

LOVE, Dave

DAVE AND RICH -
HOW COLD IS IT?

IT'S SO COLD THE PINTO WORE WOOL SOCKS INSTEAD OF TIRES.

BRRRR

IT'S SO COLD THE BIRDS COULDN'T SING BECAUSE THEIR TEETH WERE CHATTERING.

IT'S SO COLD THE BARK ON THE TREES COULDN'T BARK -- IT JUST GROWLED....

IT'S SO COLD THAT OUR CLOCK WAS RUBBING ITS HANDS TOGETHER.

IT'S SO COLD THAT THE YARDSTICK WAS STOMPING ITS FEET.

P.S. it's really not that Bad out after all

LOVE, Dad

# Good Morning, Guys,

✳ Rich, Good Luck on Your Test Today.

✳ Dave, Good Luck in Patrol, Trumpet and Especially School.

✳✳ Mom, Good Luck with All Those Cub Scouts!

I'll be thinking of the three of you at work.

...Boy, it sure is hard to work sometimes when you've got such a good family to think about.

DAVE + RICH,
YOU HAD GOOD "A"
PAPERS YESTERDAY?
ARE WE SEEING
ALL YOUR PAPERS, THE
GOOD AND THE BAD?
BRING THEM ALL HOME.
NOBODY IS PERFECT.
YOUR MOM AND I HAD
MORE THAN OUR
SHARE OF BAD PAPERS
IN SCHOOL, TOO.

WE LOVE YOU.
I'LL SEE YOU TONIGHT.
LOVE.
Dad

Good Morning,
Dave and Rich —

REMEMBER
TO LEARN
SOMETHING
NEW
TODAY.
You can tell
MOM and I
about it
at dinner.
Maybe it
will be about
early civilization,
or the stars, or
about Democracy,
or maybe Math or
writing.
   I'm sure there's
something.
   Have a good day.

Love you guys.

      LOVE,
         Dad

Dave and Rich,

Yesterday Dave learned about ICEBERGS. THEY form in areas near the North and South Pole, WHERE IT IS COLD. IF IT WEREN'T FOR ICEBERGS, THE OCEANS WOULD BE WARMER.

WELL, WHAT NEW THINGS WILL YOU TWO GUYS learn today? Now IS THE TIME TO FILL YOUR heads with LOTS OF NEW INFORMATION AND IDEAS. WHEN YOU GET A NEW IDEA, FIND OUT ALL ABOUT IT.

THAT WAY, YOU WILL KNOW MORE ABOUT HOW THE WORLD WORKS.

LOVE, Dad

Dave and Rich -
try not to be too tired
today. You were up
late last night but
it was for a good cause.

I fell asleep in class once.
My eyes closed and I
remember starting
to dream. The next thing
I knew, I had fallen out
of my seat. I hit the
floor with a **BANG!** that
woke me up. All the other
students were very
quiet and so was the
teacher, who just stared
at me until I crawled
back into my seat.

KLUNK!!

LOVE, Dad

DAVE AND RICH,

I'LL BE THINKING
ABOUT YOU TWO
TODAY.

PAY ATTENTION
IN SCHOOL.

LISTEN MORE THAN
YOU TALK.

MAKE THE WORLD
A BETTER PLACE BECAUSE
YOU'RE THERE,

LOVE,
Dad

Dave and Rich,
Mom and I THOUGHT
You Two WERE VERY GOOD
Last night AT THE
Scout Picnic. Also,
THANKS FOR THE HELP
IN GETTING AND KEEPING
IT ORGANIZED BY TOTING
EQUIPMENT, FLAGS, ROPES,
FIREWOOD. YOU BOTH
WERE A BIG HELP.
WE DIDN'T EVEN HAVE
ANY SERIOUS ACCIDENTS.

DAVE AND RICH =
I LOVE YOU
GUYS AND I'LL
BE THINKING
ABOUT YOU AT
THE OFFICE.

TRY TO LEARN
SOMETHING HARD
TODAY.

TAKE SOMETHING
YOU DON'T UNDERSTAND
AND FIGURE IT OUT.

IT FEELS GOOD
TO LEARN SOMETHING
NEW LIKE THAT.

Have a good day.

LOVE,
Dad.

Dave AND Rich,
 Have a good day
 in school.
Oh, it's report card
day.
   Well, I'm sure you two
 will do okay.
    You can get any grade,
as long as I know
you're trying.
    It's when you slough off
or get too lazy for too long
that I get concerned.
    Over all, you've both done
a good job.

            Love,

              Dad

Dave and Rich,
I SURE HAD
A GOOD WEEKEND.
I HOPE YOU DID,
TOO.
SHERI HAS A WARM,
FRIENDLY HOUSE.
EVEN COUGAR FELT
AT HOME THERE.

CHINESE FOOD TASTED
delicious last night.
SOME PEOPLE ARE
SURPRISED THAT YOU
EAT PEAPODS, BUT IT
IS TRUE. You also munch
on Bamboo shoots.

MUNCH!

CRUNCH!

"CHINESE FOOD IS
DELICIOUS,
INTERESTING,...
AND NOISY."

LOVE, Dad

DAVE AND RICH,
HAVE A GOOD DAY.
TRY TO LEARN SOMETHING NEW.
TRY TO TEACH SOMETHING VALUABLE.
TRY TO SAY SOMETHING FRIENDLY.
TRY TO DO SOMETHING WISE.

Love,
Dad

GOOD MORNING, DAVE & RICH -

RICH, YOUR PAPER IS GOOD.
DON'T FORGET THE
ICHTHYOHICCIPUS. HE WAS
75 FEET LONG. BUT WHEN
HE HICCUPED, HE STRETCHED
TO 225 FEET LONG.

REGULAR

DURING HICCUP

HICCUP!

HE ATE LEAVES OFF TREES OR SOMETIMES
SMALL CAVEMEN.

ICHTHYOHICCIPUS AND
CAVEMAN

DAVE, I FORGOT TO ASK YOU ABOUT TRUMPET
PRACTICE CLASS YESTERDAY. CALL AND TELL
ME HOW IT WENT.      LOVE, Dad

Dave and Rich —
I've BEEN THINKING
A LOT ABOUT IT AND
You two sure are
LIKABLE. You're
A GOOD TEAM. IN FACT,
WE'RE ALL A GOOD
TEAM. I DON'T KNOW
ABOUT YOU, BUT I SURE
FEEL LUCKY?

KEEP UP THE GOOD WORK.
DON'T SLOW UP AND
DON'T GIVE UP WHEN
IT GETS HARD. THAT'S
THE TIME TO STICK
WITH IT THE MOST.

MAKE A HABIT OUT OF
STICKING WITH IT.

LOVE,
Dad

Dave and Rich,
I'll see you
guys tonight.
We had a fine
night last
night with
Dave trumpeting
and Rich working
on homework.

In the background
was the flickering
fire.
Who could ask
for anything more?

Dave,
Here are some similes
to fill in:

① As big as a _____.
② The baby was soft as _____.
③ The jet engine sounded like
_____.
④ The apple was as red as _____.

I love you guys
and am proud of you.
Love,
Dad

DAVE AND RICH,
Have a good
new WEEK.
THIS IS THE
FIRST TIME
IN THE HISTORY
OF THE WHOLE
WORLD THAT THIS
WEEK HAS rolled around.
IT IS ONLY SEVEN LITTLE
DAYS LONG, SO SPEND
THEM CAREFULLY.

ALSO, TODAY ASK YOUR TEACHERS
WHETHER YOU HAVE to WORK
EXTRA HARD ON ANYTHING
TO GET AN ACCEPTABLE
REPORT CARD.

LOVE,
Dad

DAVE + RICH,
GOOD MORNING!

WORK HARD
IN SCHOOL
TODAY.
PAY ATTENTION.
LEARN MORE
ABOUT YOUR
WORLD.
YOU'RE PRETTY
LUCKY TO HAVE
TEACHERS.
MANY CHILDREN
IN THE WORLD
DON'T HAVE
TEACHERS, OR
EVEN SCHOOLS.
THEY GROW UP
AND CAN'T READ,
WRITE, ADD or
SUBTRACT. THEY
NEVER LEARN
THAT AMERICA
EXISTS... OR
ABOUT AMERICAN
CHILDREN.

LOVE,
Dad

OR AMERICAN
DOGS. MORE'S
THE PITY!

DAVE AND RICH —
Have a good learning day!

You Guys should check
to see if today is BAND
Practice.

LOVE,
Dad

Dave and Rich —

Cousin Frank WENT TO Bremerton today to VISIT UNCLE GEORGE, BUT HE'LL BE BACK Tonight.

THAT LOOKED LIKE KIND OF A HEAVY SUITCASE, DAVE. THANKS.

RICH, write the figure NINE TRILLION, two hundred and forty-three billion, four hundred and sixty-two million, three hundred and twenty-two thousand and six.

Dave, what is 925 multiplied by .00051?

LOVE, Dad

DAVE AND RICH...

I LOVE YOU AND WISH
WE COULD ALL DO SOMETHING
TOGETHER TODAY.

BUT WE'LL GO OUR
SEPARATE WAYS AND DO
WHAT WE HAVE TO.

DOING OUR DUTY AND
DOING OUR BEST
WITH A SMILE ON OUR
FACE IS A FORM OF
LOVE, TOO. IT MAKES
OTHER PEOPLE FEEL
GOOD.

LOVE,
Dad

Dave and Rich,
Have a Happy
Halloween
with all your
boy fiends
and
ghoul friends!

Dave, Good luck on your
Social Studies test.

Rich, You'll want to finish your pumpkin.
See you two tonight.

Love,

Dad

KIDS,

Good Morning.

It's cold. this morning I saw a slug with a muffler on. That's a sure sign winter is coming.

You guys have a good day.

HELP AROUND THE HOUSE.

Love,

Dad

DAVE AND RICH...

TONIGHT WE'LL GO
OUT AND GET A
PUMPKIN FOR THE
PACK MEETING.

YOU GUY'S HAVE
SWIMMING TONIGHT
IN ADDITION TO YOUR
CHORES AND ANY
HOMEWORK AND,
OF COURSE,
TRUMPET.

BOY, YOU'RE BUSY.

"IT WOULD INDUBITABLY
BE AN HONOR TO BE A
PACK 307 PUMPKIN!"

LOVE,
Dad

DAVE AND RICH---

WELL, I had a couple of nice days off, thanks to Mom and you guys.

I'M GLAD I'M Not a turkey this time of year.

We Love You Guys.

Love,

Dad

KIDS,
GOOD MORNING!
WHAT DID THE TURKEY SAY TO THE PILGRIM?

"WHY DON'T YOU
EAT THANKSGIVING
RABBIT INSTEAD?"

Why don't you try to play outside awhile
to get some fresh air.
I'll see you later.

LOVE,
Dad

DAVE & RICH

"MOM, WOULD YOU PLEASE HELP US GET OUR BREAD DOUGH ORNAMENT IN THE OVEN?"

I THINK THOSE KIDS GOT ARTISTICALLY OUT OF HAND....

LOVE, Dave

Dave and Rich
Hi. I'm a christmas butterfly.
...you know what I do?
...I FREEZE...
...If I had a choice
I'd rather be a Christmas Polar bear
And a Fourth of July Butterfly!
But I'm not only Beautiful but I'm tough and I understand the way things go so I'LL MAKE THE BEST OF WHAT I AM. MERRY CHRISTMAS!
(FLUTTER FLUTTER... SHIVER SHIVER)
LOVE, Dad

DEAR DAVE AND RICH,

ANOTHER GLISTENING CHRISTMAS
IS PAST AND NOTHING CAN
TAKE AWAY FROM CELEBRATING
THE BIRTH OF JESUS AS A
FAMILY. CHRISTMAS MORNING
WAS A BEAUTIFUL, EXCITING
TIME FOR ALL OF US.

NOT THE PRESENTS.
THEY WEREN'T IMPORTANT (EXCEPT
THE ONES A PERSON GIVES).

BUT BEING TOGETHER. THAT'S
IMPORTANT.

SHARING LOVE. DOING KIND
THINGS FOR EACH OTHER.
—THAT'S IMPORTANT.

LOOKING OUT FOR WHAT'S BEST
FOR OTHERS.
—THAT'S IMPORTANT.

CARING FOR EACH OTHER.
—THAT'S IMPORTANT.

BRINGING PEACE INTO
EACH OTHER'S LIVES.
—THAT'S IMPORTANT.

AS 1979 SHUFFLES AWAY LIKE AN
OLD MAN AND 1980 BOUNCES IN LIKE
A BABY, WE SHOULD REMEMBER
WHAT OUR CHRISTMAS MEANT
TO EACH OTHER.

LOVE,
Dad

DAVE + RICH –

HAPPY NEW YEAR!

THIS IS A TIME OF
FRESH STARTS AND
NEW BEGINNINGS.

IT IS A TIME WHEN
PEOPLE MAKE
"NEW YEAR'S RESOLUTIONS".
HAVE YOU MADE ANY?

Grandma, Mom AND I
HOPE 1980 AND THE WHOLE
DECADE OF THE 1980s
IS GOOD TO YOU.

LOVE,

Dad

P.S. YOU GUYS
SHOULD WRITE
SOME THANK-YOU
NOTES FOR
CHRISTMAS
PRESENTS.

DAVE AND RICH-

it SOUNDS AS THOUGH YOUR TEACHERS HAVE A GOOD YEAR IN STORE FOR YOU.

YOU EACH HAD GOOD PICTURES ON THE BOARD.

GOOD LUCK IN Your tests Today.

Your teachers didn't seem too scared.

SEE You tonight.

LOVE,

Dad...

Dear Kids,
Good Morning.
Have a good day
in school.
It's good that you're
nervous about the
Honor Band Concert,
Rich. It means you
want to do a good
job. We know you will!

_____

Love,
  Dad

DEAR DAVE & RICH —

DON'T WORRY ABOUT FRIENDS.
BE FAIR AND FRIENDLY AND
YOUR FRIENDS WILL COME.
THE IMPORTANT THING IS
NOT HOW MANY FRIENDS
YOU HAVE BUT WHAT KIND
OF FRIENDS. YOU HAVE VERY
GOOD FRIENDS AND AS YOU
GET OLDER, YOU'LL HAVE
MORE BECAUSE YOU ARE
A GOOD FRIEND.

LOVE,

Dad

DAVE AND RICH-
HAVE A GOOD
DAY IN SCHOOL.
WORK AT HAVING
A GOOD DAY IF
THAT'S WHAT
IT TAKES.

BE A CONTRIBUTOR
IN YOUR CLASSES.

DON'T BE A
DISTRACTOR:
THAT'S A WASTE
OF TIME.

LOVE,
Dad

DAVE and RICH,
THANK YOU BOTH
FOR THE WONDERFUL
VALENTINES. MOM
WAS KNOCKED OUT
AND BOWLED OVER
AND SO WAS I.

... THE ONLY TROUBLE
IS THAT WE HAD TO
HIRE SOME MEN FROM
A MOVING COMPANY
TO HELP US PUT THE
CARDS AWAY!

"THIS IS THE
BIGGEST DARN
VALENTINE I'VE
EVER SEEN. I LIKE
WHAT THEY SAY, TOO."

"EASY, GEORGE, WE DON'T
WANT A BROKEN HEART."

LOVE,
Dad

Dave and Rich,

Happy St. Patrick's Day! You two were a lot of help yesterday in fixing things up for the shindig. Thanks a lot.

I think leprechauns sometimes ride cougar like Gunter-Gebel Williams rides elephants. I saw one just a minute ago.

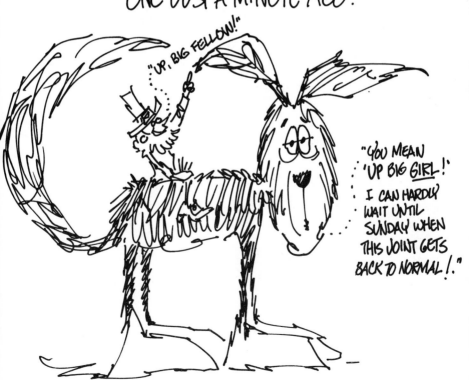

Dave and Rich -
Thanks for all
Your help with
the wood yesterday.
We will have
many warm fires
to fend off the damp
cold this winter. It
was a pleasant outing
with Mom and you
guys, driving past
the valley with the mist,
colored trees, the cattle
and the peaceful sight
of smoke lazily rising
from the chimneys:
It's also always enjoyable
to really work at something
together, like lugging those
logs around. I love you
guys. We both do. We're
very lucky.....and you two
are lucky, too.

Love,
Dad

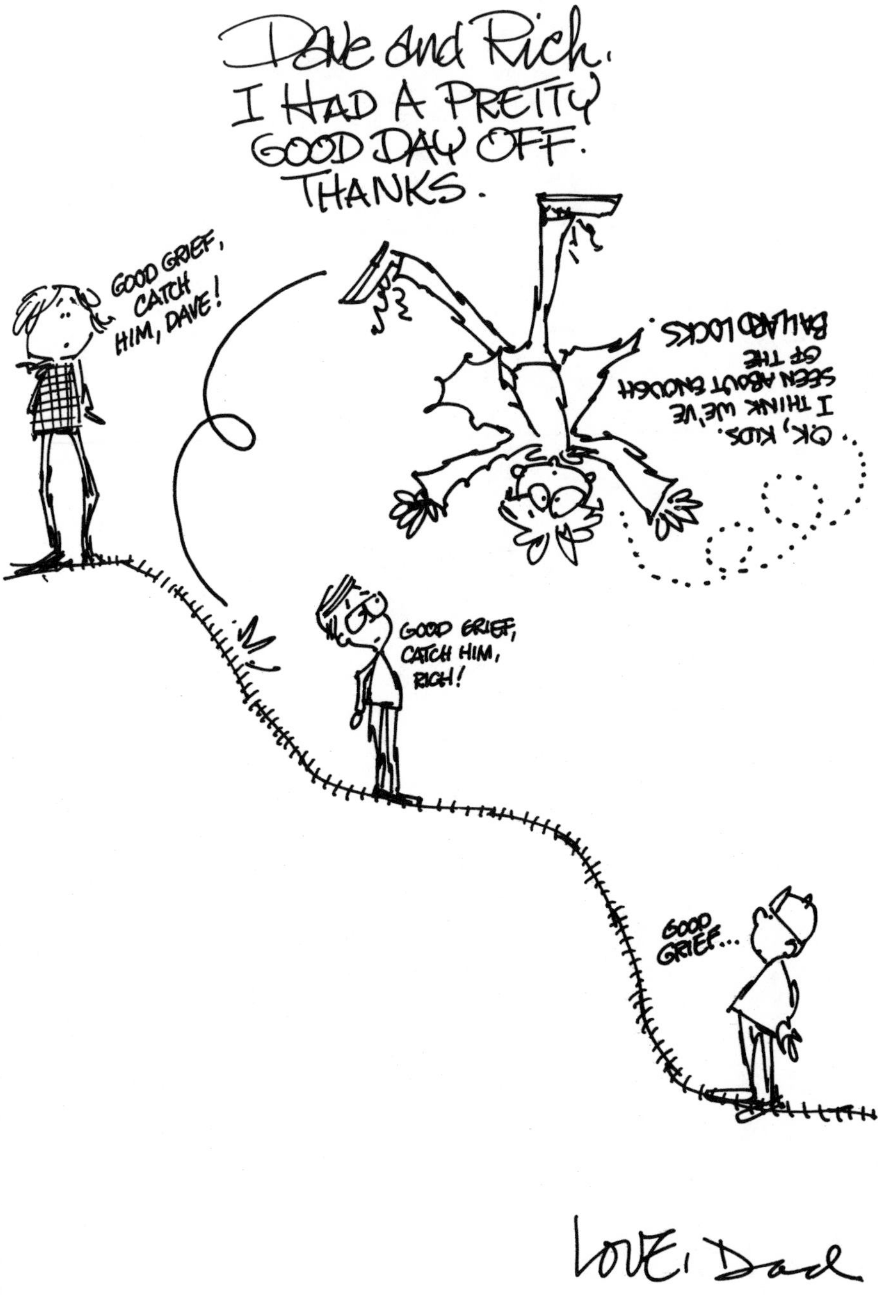
Dave and Rich,
I HAD A PRETTY GOOD DAY OFF. THANKS.
GOOD GRIEF, CATCH HIM, DAVE!
O.K., KIDS. I THINK WE'VE SEEN ABOUT ENOUGH OF THE BALLARD LOCKS.
GOOD GRIEF, CATCH HIM, RICH!
GOOD GRIEF...
LOVE, Dad

KIDS,
# HAPPY EASTER!

ABOUT 2,000 YEARS AGO, JESUS DIED ON THE CRUCIFIX FOR OUR SINS. THEN HE AROSE FROM THE DEAD ON EASTER. THAT IS WHY WE CELEBRATE EASTER. IT IS A TIME OF JOY AND A TIME TO CELEBRATE THE RETURN OF SPRING, WHEN ALL THINGS START GROWING AGAIN. IT IS A TIME WHEN PEOPLE "START OVER" AND TRY TO IMPROVE THE LITTLE AREAS OF THEMSELVES THEY WANT TO MAKE BETTER.

HAVE A GOOD DAY. BE ON YOUR BEST BEHAVIOR.

LOVE,
Dad

Dave and Rich,

MOUNT ST. HELENS
BLEW AGAIN LAST
NIGHT. THERE IS
MORE ASH FALLING
ON EASTERN
WASHINGTON, IDAHO
AND MONTANA.

Have a good day
in School!

Love,
Dad

DAVE AND RICH —
WINTER IS GONE!
IT'S SPRING!

TODAY IS THE
FIRST DAY OF
SPRING.
THAT'S THE
TIME OF YEAR
WHEN BIRDS
AND ANIMALS
HAVE BABIES
AND FLOWERS
START GROWING
ANEW.

I HOPE BOTH
YOU GUYS
HAVE A
HAPPY SPRING!

LOVE,
Dad

DAVE AND RICH
YOUR DUET
LAST NIGHT
SOUNDED GOOD.
RRRRR...
RRRRR...
R...RRR
(OR WAS IT A TRIO?)
Have a good day.
Love,
Dad

# DAVE AND RICH ~

## ☀ HAPPY FRIDAY ---

☀ IT'S ALSO FRIDAY THE 13TH, WHICH SOME PEOPLE CONSIDER UNLUCKY. BUT IT'S REALLY NO LUCKIER OR UNLUCKIER THAN ANY OTHER DAY. A LOT OF IT DEPENDS ON YOU.

☀ Mount St. Helens blew again last night. It sent a plume of steam and ash more than 50,000 feet into the air. Some ash fell in Vancouver and Portland. It was the biggest eruption since the blast May 18 that flattened all those trees and killed so many people.

LOVE,
Dad

DAVE AND RICH,

Vacation is over for me and soon
you will be going back to school.
It can be a very interesting,
exciting year for both of you.
You've learned a lot in your
travels that can be shared.
You've both grown in mind
as well as body And you're
both ready to go onto the
next step in your life.
Mom and I will help you
make it a good step.

You
can do
it!

Love,
Dad

Dave and Rich.

**MOM AND I WILL ALWAYS**
**BE HERE WHEN YOU NEED US.**

That does not mean we will
baby you or pamper you.
It does not mean we will let
you be lazy. It does not mean
you can be thoughtless or
selfish where other people are
concerned. But it means
we love you and will do everything we can to see that you
grow up straight, honest, hard-
working, generous, and full
of a sense of wonder and a
sense of humor.

Mom and I are looking
forward to that.

LOVE,
Dad

Dave and Rich,
Sorry I keep
missing you.
I'll bet you've
grown since the
last time I saw
you.

"MY BOYS ARE GROWING A BIT."

Love,
Dad

DAVE AND RICH -

# Another day!

You two can learn a lot if you pay attention and treat your teachers and fellow students with respect. Remember the GOLDEN RULE. Ask Mom what that means.

I'LL BE THINKING ABOUT BOTH OF YOU TODAY AND HOPING YOU'RE DOING WELL. Mom AND I WILL HELP YOU WITH ANYTHING.

Love,
Dad

I love You Guys!

DAVE AND RICH-

LISTEN ON THE
ROOF AND THE GRASS—
IT'S GOOD, OLD-FASHIONED
SEATTLE RAIN
SPLATTERING DOWN.
IT SOUNDS LIKE
LOTS OF IT.

THE RADIO SAYS
SOME SCHOOLS ARE
CLOSED BECAUSE
OF SNOW.

BUT WE JUST GOT
PLAIN RAIN... WHICH
WAS A DRAIN ON THE
WINDOW PANE... THAT
DROVE COUGAR INSANE...

I LOVE YOU GUYS,

LOVE,
Dad

P.S. HAPPY UNBIRTHDAY
TO BOTH OF YOU!

DAVE AND RICH—

Have a good learning day!

RICH, Maybe you need some extra help in MATH and SPELLING. We can do it with you.

You Guys check the time of the next band practice.

Love,

Dad

DAVE AND RICH
You two sure sounded good
on your trumpets
last night. Keep practicing
to make it even better.
Pay attention in school
to improve your brains.
ASK FOR HELP WHEN
YOU DON'T UNDERSTAND
SOMETHING. DON'T WASTE
TIME. BE COURTEOUS
TO YOUR TEACHERS
AND CLASSMATES.

love,

Dave

"I am lucky to be free
  of that dad-blamed scratchy flea
  and his PESKY Brothers and sisters
  who HOP around My fur and whiskers.
    My doctor smiled and said you guys
  were the ones who won for me
      the prize
  of "FLEA FREE DOG" in his flea
      check
  for hopping critters from knee
      to neck.
To you two Guys I give my all,
I beg, I bow, I sing, I crawl,
I roll, I come, I spit, I jump —
My FLEAS HAVE FLED TO THE
County dump!!!

"THANK YOU...THANK YOU...
I LIKE TO HAVE AN
OCCASIONAL READING
OF MY POETRY TO BRING A
LITTLE CLASS TO THIS JOINT...."

Dave and Rich—

WHAT A NIGHT! Dave showed his stuff at the roller rink and Rich won 2 FIRST-PRIZE ribbons for his costume!!

Dave,    A Boy named Clamshare Biddlespoon DEVOTED all his attention to his pet mole.

That means Clamshare, a serious little fellow,

A.) Ignored his pet mole.

B.) forgot his pet mole.

C.) Ate his pet mole at breakfast.

D.) Gave all his attention to his pet mole.

E.) Loaned his pet mole to his mother to help with lawn work.

F.) Took his pet mole for a walk because it wasn't housebroken.

G.) Accidentally stepped on his pet mole.

Put correct letter of ANSWER here

LOVE, Dad

KIDS,

GOOD MORNING.

A GUY GETS KIND OF TIRED WORKING.

THE ELECTION.

THE BAGS UNDER MY EYES HAVE BAGS UNDER THEM.

I HOPE YOU HAD A GOOD NIGHT WITH MOM. I KNOW GRANDMA LIKED HEARING FROM YOU FOR HER BIRTHDAY.

Please come in AND SEE ME BEFORE YOU TAKE OFF FOR SCHOOL.

LOVE,

Dad

DAVE AND RICH ~

BE SURE TO LISTEN
TO WHAT OTHER KIDS
DID OVER THEIR
VACATIONS.
THEN YOU CAN TELL WHAT
YOU DID.
BUT REMEMBER TO BE
A GOOD LISTENER
FIRST.

LOVE,
Dad

DAVE AND RICH,

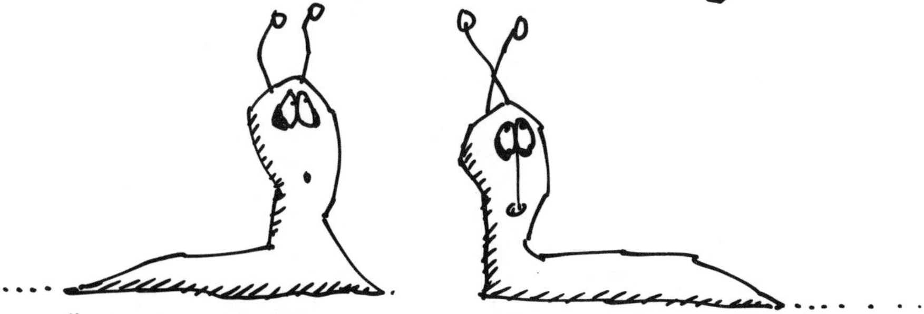

"BOY, GEORGE, I'VE NEVER SEEN SO MANY SLUGS."

"I THINK I SAW A COUPLE OF DIRTY SOCKS, TOO, ALBERT."

KIDS,

PLEASE EXCUSE THE BAD PUNS!

LOVE YOU,

Dad

DAVE AND RICH,

It's another new week, even if it's an abbreviated one for school.

What does abbreviated mean? Can you figure it out?

A nickel to each of you if you can figure it out and use it in a sentence. You can use the dictionary.

RICH, work on your Minnesota report. Remember to include your personal observations. You already know quite a bit about Minnesota by visiting Grandpa and Grandma.

DAVE, your first poster looks good, but if you haven't finished the second one, get cracking.

Love,
Dad

DAVE AND RICH

"I THINK I'M GETTING THE KNACK OF JUGGLING, RICH."

"OUCH! NOT QUITE SOON ENOUGH, DAVE!"

LOVE,

Dave

DAVE AND RICH,

IT WAS JUST A
WEEK AGO THAT
GOD PUT ON THE
ECLIPSE. WHAT
A SIGHT THAT
WAS! I'M
THRILLED THAT
MOM DROVE
200 MILES
SO YOU COULD
SEE IT.

I'LL BE THINKING
ABOUT YOU TWO
GUYS — AND YOUR
PRETTY MOM —
TODAY AT WORK.

LOVE,
Dad

DAVE & RICH—

I HOPE YOU GUYS
HAVE A GOOD DAY.

DAVE, YOU ESPECIALLY
BE HELPFUL THIS
MORNING, SINCE
YOU'LL PROBABLY
BE UP ON MOUNT
RAINIER TONIGHT
SCARING BEARS.

YOU HAD BETTER
HOPE THAT MOUNT
RAINIER DOESN'T
ERUPT. YOU KNOW
WHO'D GET THE
BLAME.

RICH, HAVE A GOOD
DAY. YOUR AIRPLANE
Model looks good!

I LOVE YOU GUYS
AND I LOVE MOM
VERY MUCH.
I'M VERY LUCKY.

LOVE,
Dad

## About the Author

Patrick Joseph Connolly was born St. Patrick's Day, 1942, in Minneapolis. After graduating from the Journalism School of the University of Minnesota in 1964, he headed west to his first job with the *Billings* (Mont.) *Gazette*. He met his wife, Laura, in Montana, and they were married in 1967.

Pat and Laura made the Northwest their home when Pat joined the Seattle Bureau of the Associated Press and they adopted two boys, David and Richard. Because the Connollys lived outside of Seattle — in Edmonds — Pat usually left for work before their boys were up. As Pat and Laura ate breakfast, he wrote an illustrated note to his sons ... with love. He did this every working day, and Laura kept them all.

Connolly was a skilled political writer and analyst who was admired by his peers for his interviewing technique. He particularly enjoyed doing human interest features, writing with warmth and compassion about people, the less important as well as the great. He was a good photographer and an excellent cartoonist and caricaturist. While interviewing, he often made small (not always flattering) caricatures of his subject, which he would then ask to have autographed for his own collection. These include Gerald Ford, Lillian Carter, Dixie Lee Ray, Red Skelton, Jerry Brown, Henry Kissinger, and Mary Martin.

Pat Connolly died at age 41 of a massive heart attack that was complicated by diabetes. Through this book — and the memory of those who knew, respected, and loved him — Pat Connolly's exuberance for life lives on.